THE GALE & POLDEN TRAINING SERIES

HOUSE TO HOUSE FIGHTING

By

COLONEL G. A. WADE, M.C.

AUTHOR OF

" The Defence of Bloodford Village," etc.

The Naval & Military Press Ltd

Published by

The Naval & Military Press Ltd

Unit 5 Riverside, Brambleside
Bellbrook Industrial Estate
Uckfield, East Sussex
TN22 1QQ England

Tel: +44 (0)1825 749494

www.naval-military-press.com
www.nmarchive.com

SUMMARY

BETTER TRAINING, FEWER CASUALTIES.
> Ignorance—Blood.
> Tanks hate houses.

BEWILDERING BUSINESS.
> No two problems alike.
> Difficult to make plan.

SIMPLIFICATION AND ANALYSIS.
> Finest sport on earth?
> British excel in it?
> You will love it.
> Play hell with bloody Huns?

HENRY FORD.
> Split it into little jobs.

FIRST PRINCIPLE.
> **Clearly defined objective.** (Give examples.)
> Patrol should not be sent into blue.
> Clear-cut—definite—known to all.
> Discretion.

SECOND PRINCIPLE.
> **Guard against surprise.**
> Extreme liability to surprise.
> Surprise **the enemy.**
> Houses splendid cover.
> Every house a passage.
> Use of scouts.
> No need to creep.
> Shots are fired.

THIRD PRINCIPLE.
> **Never advance without covering fire.**
> **Kill** enemy without **being killed.**
> **Adequate** covering fire.

2

Look down **Our Street.**
Hun on **right** (Plate 1).
Hun on **left.**
Which side would **you** get?
Expect more enemy on **right.**
Make him **show** himself.
Try aiming out of window.

HOW SCOUTS ACT.

Hunting in pairs (Plate 2).
Scouts **bounds**—Patrol **steady progress.**
Factors affecting numbers used.
Found equally from each section.

LET US FOLLOW SCOUT.

How to look round corner (Plate 13).
Sly dog! Another look.
" No enemy in sight."
Slow deliberation—sudden spurts.
" Hound on the trail." Second scout.
" Enemy in sight in **small numbers.**"
Another look—**large** numbers.
Second scout passes signals.
Well done—Warned patrol.
Without alarming enemy !
Distance of scouts from patrol.
Second scout must keep touch both ways.

CLEARING A STREET (PLATE 7).

Not feasible to attack rear in this case.

First, DEFINE OBJECTIVE.

Second, ARRANGE COVERING FIRE.

Third, ATTACK WITH SPEED.

Describe method.

ACTION OF No. 2 SECTION.

Equipment—helmets—bayonets—S.A.A. in pockets.
Gumboots—silence—do not slip.

3   H TO H

Mills grenades—crowbar—sledge-hammer.
No more till **covering fire** ready.
Bashing in doors—correct way.
" They would bunch round doors " (Plate 8).
Procedure indoors—start on cellars.
Every man knows his job.
Use of Mills grenades.
Enemy upstairs.
Upward covering fire.
" Damage his morale."
Three prisoners.
Attack next house.

OTHER METHODS.

From the roof.
Through cockloft.
Through walls.
Cellar to cellar.

ATTACKING HOUSES.

Do not use too many men.
Keep reserves under cover.
All should know plan.
Always **press on.**
Trip wires useful.
Do not **lose momentum.**
Party cannot provide own covering fire.
Place covering party in **right place.**
Use gardens.
Position of Leader.
Keep enemy on jump.
Study windows.
Use of smoke—crossing street.
Use of explosives—Study of maps.
Barricades—Northover—Smoke.

DEFENDING HOUSES.

Attack is **best** defence.
Which way will Hun come?

4

Occupy roof—Fire from unexpected places.
Do not let muzzle show.
Guard against hand grenades.
Fire fighting.
Stout cellars—Barricade doors—Connect houses.
Bullet-proof cover.
Every man to know his job.
Keen observation—Shooting from both shoulders.
Booby traps.

MUTUAL SUPPORT (PLATE 14).
Explain example.
Applies to town houses also.

LITTLE THINGS WHICH MATTER.
Trip wires give warning.
Barbed and Dannert wire in entries.
Make a trap.
Use of bombs—be careful.
Do not start a fire.
Know where to dart.
Do not let bayonet show.

COMMON FAULTS:—

LACK OF DETERMINATION.
Plan not made clear—faulty training.
Too much use of cover.

LACK OF COHESION.
Men spread out into couples.
Wide separation.
Pincer movements not synchronized.
Enemy takes on each party in turn !
Due to bad arrangement of tasks.
Bad timing—unexpected situations.
Push on whatever happens.
Signal for final charge.

LACK OF WARINESS.
Attention on enemy—surprised.
Caught in cul-de-sac.

5

Shouting—talking—crashing about.
Lack of **imagination.**
Bad leadership.
Carelessness and bad training.

SCOUTS SHOULD ALWAYS BE POSTED.

STREET FIGHTING COMPETITION (Plate 15).
Information.
Task.
Winner took forty-five minutes.

LESSONS.
Terrible tendency to split up.
Must have **punch at the end.**
Speed of paramount importance.
Keep close together until fired upon.
Scouts should be sent out instantly.
Quietness essential—loud issue of orders.
Adequate look-out.
Solution of problem.

TANKS IN TOWNS.
Assail them by every weapon.
Shot-gun—Pig-like eyes.
Slow it down—screens and obstacles.
Keep it up !
After dark.
Keep above or below it.
Do not worry if one gets past.
Get ready for next.
Fight and **fight** and fight.

FINISH.
Knowledge and practice.
See your enemy in every nook and corner.

HOUSE-TO-HOUSE FIGHTING IS REALLY A GREAT GAME.

6

HOUSE TO HOUSE FIGHTING

A FASCINATING PROBLEM

IN all kinds of fighting the better the training of the men engaged the fewer the casualties, but in that fierce form of warfare where determined men encounter each other in built-up areas it is no exaggeration to say that losses sustained by untrained troops will be more than *ten times* what they would have been had they known their job.

Ignorance has to be paid for in blood.

Now that tanks tend to dominate the battlefield, fighting in or near houses is likely to increase in frequency and intensity. You see, tanks hate houses because if they get close to them they become hemmed in, A.W. bombs may be thrown from upstairs windows and mines slipped under the tracks. The tank's guns will not elevate sufficiently to hit high windows and will not depress enough to shoot a man creeping from an entry; road blocks and flame-throwers may be encountered unexpectedly and the advantage passes to the defence. In other words, the awe-inspiring tank loses all its magic in a street and becomes just a lumbering iron contraption awaiting final preparation for the salvage dump.

At first glance fighting amongst houses seems a bewildering business, and no two tactical problems look alike. The arrangement of the houses, their size, height and relative positions all appear to vary in different parts. Streets are all widths and degrees of straightness, and entries, gardens, squares, side streets, culs-de-sac, etc., provide infinite variety. Consequently when word is received that an enemy in unknown strength is somewhere amongst it all it seems extremely difficult to decide on a plan either for attack or defence.

But, in spite of its forbidding appearance, house-to-house fighting is capable of simplification and analysis, and it is possible to apply certain general principles which will quickly point the way to a good plan of action which can be followed with complete confidence.

Do you know that house-to-house fighting is the finest sport on earth?

Do you know that it is just the sort of close-quarter scrapping we British excel in?

Do you know that once you get going you will *love* it?

Do you want to come with me down our street and play hell with some bloody Huns?

You do? Right, we'll carry on!

II

DEFINING THE TASK

The wise saying of Henry Ford that, no matter how big a job is, it becomes easy if you split it into a lot of little jobs applies very forcibly to house-to-house fighting—in fact, it gives us our first guiding principle:—

EVERY DETACHMENT MUST HAVE A CLEARLY DEFINED OBJECTIVE

Such as:—

"You will capture and consolidate SOUTH side of HIGH STREET from BUCK INN to the POST OFFICE."

Or:—

"You will turn enemy out of THE GRANGE and THERE AWAIT FURTHER ORDERS."

Or:—

"You will clear all houses on this side of the road from here to the CROSS-ROADS and wait there under cover till relieved by 'B' Company."

Or:—

"You will retake the triangle of houses bounded by the CANAL, the MARKET-PLACE and the RAILWAY."

8

The task given a fighting patrol should be well within its power and clearly defined by some easily recognizable features.

If it can be avoided, a patrol should never be sent off into the blue on a vague errand, but its job should be *clear cut, definite* and *known* to all the men.

(NOTE.—This does *not* mean that the Patrol Leader must not exercise his discretion. For instance:—

Enemy might not be in the house he had been ordered to attack, but have moved to next one. In that case, of course, leader would not hesitate to act accordingly.)

III

AVOIDING CASUALTIES

Having fixed a definite task, what is the next guiding principle we must apply?

GUARD AGAINST SURPRISE

House-to-house fighting lends itself to sudden surprise situations and the object of the patrol is not only to avoid being surprised but to *surprise the enemy.*

There is splendid cover in houses. A score of men may be in a house and no aeroplane can spot them, and the whole lot may come charging out of doorways, windows, gateways and entries to catch the patrol unawares.

Every house in a town is a passage and every window a loophole from which death may come.

Consequently, the patrol must move circumspectly with scouts in front of it, scouts covering its flanks, and scouts watching its rear. In this formation the patrol can cover ground quickly and confidently. There is no need for the patrol to creep on its belly (as if wishing to apologize to Hitler for being on the earth) until the enemy is definitely located either by our scouts spotting them or by shots being fired.

Then, we come to our next guiding principle:—

NEVER ADVANCE WITHOUT ADEQUATE COVERING FIRE

Your object in house-to-house fighting is to kill the enemy without getting killed yourself. Consequently, you should aim to be as difficult a target as you can whilst compelling the enemy to expose himself to the maximum when he tries to shoot at you.

And *before* compelling him to expose himself you make sure that somebody with a straight eye is in a position to crack down on him the instant he appears.

That is what is meant by *adequate covering fire.*

Now I will take you where you can look straight down Our Street, but don't expose yourself too much because there are some Germans in it. You see the one peeping out of the window on the right-hand side of the street? He is not exposing himself much, although he is aiming in our direction. That is because he need only show his

PLATE 1

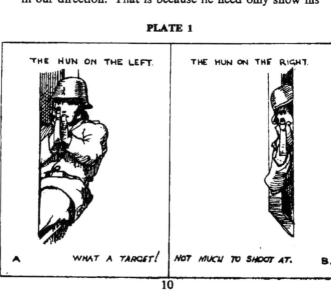

A — THE HUN ON THE LEFT. — WHAT A TARGET!

NOT MUCH TO SHOOT AT. — THE HUN ON THE RIGHT. — B.

right shoulder and half his square head in order to shoot at us. Consequently he is not a very good target for our covering fire (Plate 1B).

But look at the Boche on the left-hand side of the street. What a difference! To aim in this direction he has to expose all his head and all his chest! Give me a rifle, somebody! (Plate 1A.)

Now, I ask you, if you were expecting to be attacked which position would you take up? The one on the *right*? Of course you would! So would the Germans.

Consequently always expect more enemy *on the right of the street* than on the left because the enemy usually knows which way your attack will come from and disposes himself accordingly.

Of course, if you can do something to make him think you are going to attack up the street from one direction and then, instead of doing that, attack from the other end your covering party will have a grand time because most of the Boches will be on the wrong side and consequently will have to lean right out of the windows to shoot at you.

IV

MAKING HIM SHOW HIMSELF

The next thing to remember is : —

KEEP CLOSE TO THE ENEMY'S SIDE OF THE STREET

This compels him to lean right out to the fullest extent before he can aim at you so that he will be easy meat for the covering party before he can fire a shot.

(Get a rifle and try aiming out of a window in various directions and imagine a crack shot is aiming at *you*. This will soon give you the underlying idea.)

from each of the three sections because if they were all drawn from one section it would be so weakened that it could not carry out its function in attack or defence as laid down in " The Fighting Patrol."*

You will notice how the scouts are disposed to cover all the streets round the patrol. The main body and the scouts both cover the same distance in the same time, but in very different style: the former advances steadily and unhesitatingly, but the scouts peep very carefully from a good look-out spot, have a look round and then if all is clear select another point to bound to and move there *at the double*.

Very good men should be chosen for forward scouts, otherwise the progress of the patrol is going to be far too slow (and slowness is the besetting sin of all fighting patrols).

Let us follow a forward scout, keeping just behind him to see how he " does his stuff " till he makes contact with the enemy: —

First he runs across the main street and lies flat to look round the corner into the side street. Look how slowly he pushes his eye round the corner, how carefully he scans the windows, the roofs, and the road, looking for any signs of movement or tell-tale shadows. Sly dog! He pulls his head back, waits a few seconds and then has another look. Ah! He has decided that there is no enemy that way and is standing up ready to go across. See how clearly he makes the signal " *No enemy in sight* " (rifle held up at full extent of arm, muzzle uppermost).

Now he is running across the side street like a rabbit and making his way down the main street. All the time he is concentrating hard, his mind never wanders for a second and his eyes dart everywhere. His progress is a curious combination of slow deliberation and sudden spurts, and, like a hound on the trail, his pal, the second scout, never loses sight of him. Right down the street he goes, scrutinizing every house, entry and side street,

---

* " The Fighting Patrol," published by Gale & Polden, 1s. net.

PLATE 4

NO ENEMY IN SIGHT

PLATE 5

ENEMY IN SIGHT IN SMALL NUMBERS.

H TO H

PLATE 2

HOW THE SCOUTS PROTECT THE PATROL

You will observe that the scouts are linked together in the sketch.

This is because scouts always work in pairs within sight of one another.

The patrol is marching steadily on (with broken step). Scout A1 is about to advance and A2 will take his place *at the double*. Scout B1 then moves into A2's place, and B2 runs to occupy B1's place. C1 and C2 act similarly, and so on through the town.

The continuous red lines indicate where the scouts can see *and* shoot.

EVERY STREET IS COVERED.

12

HOW THE SCOUTS ACT

Plate 2 shows a patrol proceeding through a town. Observe the progress of the scouts, who move by bounds from one point of vantage to another. The patrol itself makes *steady progress,* relying on the protection of the scouts and does not move by bounds unless under enemy fire.

The number of scouts the patrol throws out depends entirely on the nature of the locality in which it is operating. Sometimes a pair in front and a pair in the rear will be adequate. Other times there may be a lot of alleys and side streets which will call for flank scouts in addition.

Usually the scouts will be provided in equal numbers

PLATE 3

PATROL MOVING ALONG STREET
Two scouts well in advance. Two on left of road watching windows and doors on right. You can just see one of the two rear scouts.

13

but always pushing on quickly in the safe places and slowly in the doubtful ones.

Did you notice why the scout left the wall and walked in the road? To avoid the noise which walking over that glass and rubbish would have made.

Why has he stopped?

I wonder if he hears something in that next side street? He has tip-toed to the corner and is looking carefully round. By Jove, he did not look long! See, he is holding his rifle above his head at the full extent of his arm and parallel with the ground, muzzle pointing to the front. That means " *Enemy in sight in small numbers.*"

He is having another look and now he is making the same signal again, but raising and lowering his rifle. which means " *Enemy in sight in large numbers.*"

He is also signalling " Double." It looks as if the Germans will come round the corner any moment now.

The second scout has passed the signals on to the patrol (with whom he has been careful to maintain touch) and both scouts have darted into houses. The patrol has taken cover in those shops ready to ambush the enemy.

Well done, forward scout! You have warned the patrol in time *without alarming the enemy!*

* * *

Regarding the distance scouts should be from the main body of the patrol; this will vary tremendously according to visibility, nature of the houses, streets, etc., but the general tendency is for scouts to remain *too close* to the main body.

If they do this they are not much use, because they do not spot the enemy in time to protect the patrol against surprise.

On the other hand, if they get too far away they will lose touch.

16

The second scout of each pair must keep in touch with the patrol *and* the first scout, so that if the former goes ahead too fast the second scout should halt him for a few moments.

Sometimes the main body of the patrol will move down a narrow street with half the men on one side and half on the other.

PLATE 6

ENEMY IN SIGHT IN LARGE NUMBERS

CLEARING A STREET

You have seen how the scouts are used; now let us watch a patrol execute a simple task—to clear the enemy out of houses on both sides of a street. The backs of these houses, by the way, are just back yards with high walls between them so that it is not feasible to attack the rear of the houses (Plate 7).

Here are the ORDERS:—

First—DEFINE THE OBJECTIVE

" You will clear enemy out of the houses on both sides of High Street up to the cross-roads."

Second—ARRANGE THE COVERING FIRE

" No. 1 Section will give covering fire from Houses A and B."

" No. 2 Section will take up position at X."

" No. 3 Section will take up position at Y."

Third—ATTACK WITH SPEED

" As soon as No. 1 Section is ready, No. 2 Section will advance round the corner and enter House No. 1. After clearing this, they will carry on to the next house, and so on to the cross-roads. At the same time, No. 3 Section will act in a similar way on the left side of the street. As soon as No. 3 Section has cleared half the street, covering party from A will move to A1, and as soon as practicable afterwards covering party from B will move to B1 to give closer support. The reserve will keep under cover till required. Nos. 2 and 3 Sections will each leave two scouts to prevent a surprise attack in the rear and also to shoot any enemy escaping from back of houses. I shall be with the covering party at A.

" Any questions? *Move !* "

18

PLATE 7

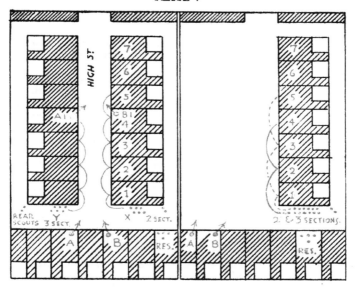

CLEARING A STREET

No. 1 Section gives *covering fire.*

No. 2 Section clears houses on right of street from house to house as shown.

No. 3 Section clears left of street in the same way.

Notes

(1) REAR SCOUTS cover entry and protect rear of Section.

(2) RESERVE is close to but under cover.

(3) When half the street is cleared COVERING PARTY would advance to A1 and B1. A must be in position at A1 before B moves.

CLEARING A ROW OF HOUSES

In this case two Sections are available for clearing Houses 1 to 7, consequently the Sections "leapfrog" up the street.

No. 2 Section takes Houses 1, 3, 5, 7, and No. 3 Section Houses 2, 4, 6.

Notes

(1) It is here possible to give covering fire from a better angle.

(2) The covering party would not advance during the clearing operation.

19

FIGHTING INDOORS

You have seen how the scouts work and have heard the orders given to the fighting patrol. Let us keep with No. 2 Section and see how it " does its stuff."

First of all, see how lightly they are equipped. Steel helmets, fixed bayonets, S.A.A. in pockets. You will notice that they are all wearing gumboots or canvas shoes. There are two reasons for that. Firstly, that *silence* is at times all-important in house-to-house fighting, and, secondly, that if the men have to run across open spaces and stop suddenly at the other side, hobnailed boots slip on the pavements and cause nasty falls. The bulges in their pockets are Mills grenades and, as you see, two men are without rifles but carry a heavy sledge-hammer and a large crowbar instead. These are for bashing in doors and breaking through walls.

The Section Leader is waiting till he gets the signal that the covering party is ready. The Patrol Leader is an experienced man and will not send any of his men into the occupied street till he knows that the very second any German tries to shoot at them he will be fired upon with deadly accuracy. The last thing in the world he will allow is an enemy to take leisurely aim at his men, so he will not let them move until he is certain about the covering fire. There, the Section Leader has got the signal, round the corner dash the door-smashers and crack! crack! go the rifles of the covering party. Watch how these two men break open the doors. They never stand in front of a closed door, for fear someone inside shoots through it, but they stand on one side and hit it obliquely. The Section Leader watches them round the corner, and the *instant the door breaks open* he sends forward the men to enter the house, but he kept them in safety till he knew they could get right inside.

A lot of casualties are incurred in house-to-house fighting by men rushing up to a house, finding the door closed and clustering round it till it is burst open. While

PLATE 8

THEY WOULD BUNCH ROUND DOORS

they are gathered there they are an easy target for enemies down the street or even inside the house (Plate 8).

Anyway, there was no delay on the threshold here, and the section are inside the house. How will they proceed now? First the Leader posts a look-out just inside the front door to make sure no Germans sally forth from one of the other houses to attack the section in the rear. Then he posts a man to prevent anyone coming downstairs and the rest of the section starts to clear the ground floor and the cellars, working in pairs with one man covering the other. If there is reason to think the enemy is in occupation of a room it is bad form to invade his privacy without previously handing in your visiting card (in the form of a Mills grenade).

Hand grenades are freakish things, and all of the enemy may not be incapacitated, but they are bound to be shaken for a second or two. The instant the bomb

21

bursts dash into the room and, if any of the occupants still has any totalitarian tendencies left, let him have the bayonet.

Now they have satisfied themselves that there are no enemy in the cellars or anywhere on the ground floor, but it is known that several enemy are upstairs, as they have been heard moving about overhead. The Section Leader is evidently considering his plan of campaign. He knows that, where it can be managed, it is better to get on the roof and work downwards. This applies more to larger buildings with flat roofs. In this case, even if men could get on to the roof without being shot by the Germans down the street, they would have difficulty in entering, so the Leader is going to attack up the stairs—not a very attractive proposition, but here again good covering fire can be given. How? Why, by firing up through the ceilings and floors. The modern rifle bullet has terrific penetrative powers and will fly through plaster and floorboarding with the

PLATE 9

ATTACK THROUGH FLOOR

PLATE 10

ATTACK THROUGH WALL

greatest ease. Consequently, rapid fire up through the
ceilings and floors will be a great shock to the Hun
above and very damaging to his morale. (In fact, a
well-aimed upward shot may damage considerably
more than his morale!)

Two men are now ready to dash upstairs, but how
quiet the whole party has gone! They are listening for
signs of the enemy on the floor above—a creaking board
may show exactly where to fire. Rifles are pointing to
the ceilings and the Leader shouts " Fire! "

Crack! crack! crack! What a din and smoke and
dust! See, the two bayonet men have bounded up the
stairs and are on the landing! Up go the rest of the
party except one man left on the watch in the hall.

Now the Leader shouts out in a savage voice:
" Come out, you ——s! "

Almost at once quavering voices say " Kamerad."
How disappointing! Three Boches appear with their
hands up. Notice how they are put facing the wall and

23

are kept covered by two men while the rest dash through the rooms looking for more.

The Leader now frisks them for weapons and sends them back under escort to the reserve.

Immediately the sledge-hammer and crowbar men are getting ready to attack the next house. And that is how it is done! All according to a definite plan, with determination and speed, with men working in pairs and with covering fire always ready. That is the way to mop up the Hun with the absolute minimum of casualties.

VIII

METHODS OF ATTACK

Where the enemy is very well organized and has all entrances to the house covered by fire it is better to attack him in some way other than from outside in the street.

THE ATTACK FROM THE ROOF

If a building has a flat roof it is always wise to occupy it. Grenades can be dropped through skylights and windows, even down chimneys, and the enemy is at a considerable disadvantage if an attack comes from above him. By occupying the roof you also cut off the enemy's escape and prevent reinforcements reaching him that way. It is usually a good place from which to direct covering fire.

THE ATTACK THROUGH THE COCKLOFT

Sometimes there is no division between semi-detached houses. If ·you attack this way take a torch and tread very quietly and carefully, remembering what has just been pointed out about bullets from below.

THE ATTACK THROUGH THE WALLS

This is much easier than it sounds (thanks to the modern jerry builder). Get the crowbar man to start

PLATE 11

ATTACK THROUGH COCK-LOFT

PLATE 12

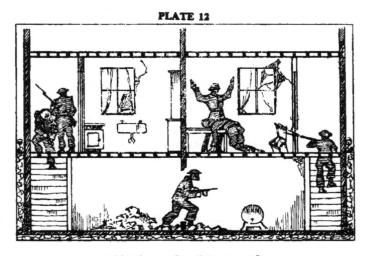

ATTACK THROUGH CELLAR

by knocking a brick out five feet from the floor. Then stick a Mills grenade through the hole; wait till it bursts and then bash a hole through and enter as quickly as possible. Incidentally, it makes you look silly if you knock a hole in the dividing wall and the Boche puts a grenade through on your side *first*; but it amuses your pals and makes them think of something flippant for your tombstone. To stop this, keep the crowbar in the hole till you are ready with *your* bomb, then pull the bar out, slip the bomb through and put the crowbar in again. It takes two to do this properly.

(NOTE.—Dividing walls are frequently thinner upstairs and also behind fireplaces.)

In certain circumstances communication from cellar to cellar may be best; and if the enemy has been in occupation of adjoining houses long enough you will find he has already made some means of inter-communication, probably between cellars.

IX

ATTACKING HOUSES

DO NOT USE TOO MANY MEN

Employ as few men as possible, remembering that a few well-trained, energetic men under firm control will accomplish more than a much larger number employed loosely.

KEEP RESERVES UNDER COVER

Men not actually taking part in the attack MUST BE KEPT UNDER COVER. If this is not done there will be more casualties from snipers amongst the *reserves* than are sustained by the *attacking* party!

MEN SHOULD ALL KNOW PLAN

Plan of attack should be known to all the men and they should be told that whatever happens they are to PUSH ON till objective is taken.

ALWAYS PRESS ON

Remember that steady progress by the attackers in spite of opposition soon demoralizes the enemy, particularly in house fighting where he feels penned in. Press on and his fire will get wild and inaccurate, and he will not wait for you to get to close quarters.

TRIP WIRES ARE USEFUL

Where possible, particularly at night, place trip wires across where he will bolt and have a couple of bayonet men handy. They may get some sport.

DON'T LOSE MOMENTUM

The Leader should do his utmost to prevent the attack losing its momentum. If it does it is always very difficult to overcome its inertia and get it going again. I consider that an attacking party has lost its momentum if it is tied down to cover and is exchanging grenades or shots with the enemy instead of pushing on to close quarters. The moment you lose momentum look out for casualties.

ADVANCE PARTY CANNOT PROVIDE ITS OWN COVERING FIRE

It is a big mistake to imagine that a patrol or section moving up an enemy-occupied street can provide its own covering fire. It cannot.

Covering fire should be *instantaneous* and *accurate* or it will be no protection at all. No man can, when walking up a street, suddenly spot a German, stop, aim and press quickly enough to prevent the enemy firing. The very fact that a man is walking up a street means that he must occasionally take his eyes away from where the enemy may be to look where he is going and that may well be the FATAL SECOND.

PLACE COVERING PARTY IN RIGHT PLACE

The correct disposition of the covering party is more than half the battle. Marksmen should be in dominating positions, such as roofs, upstairs windows, town halls, factories, etc., where they have nothing at all to do but remain comfortable and WATCH OVER THEIR SIGHTS for the enemy.

USE GARDENS IF YOU CAN

Very frequently it is better to take advantage of the cover furnished by gardens and buildings to attack the backs of houses. It all depends on circumstances, but do not make the mistake of thinking that because you attack the back of the houses you are thereby taking the enemy in the rear. It does not follow. The back of the house may be the enemy's *front*.

POSITION OF THE LEADER

The Leader of the Patrol should be in some place where there is a good view. He will not lead the patrol in the attack unless the patrol as a BODY is making an attack on ONE objective. His whereabouts should be known to the Section Leaders and their men, and he should be fairly close to the reserve.

KEEP HIM ON THE JUMP

Any invader in this country will be sparing of ammunition because his future supplies are more than problematical; consequently, if you can get him to waste it by means of dummies, etc., by all means do so.

A good way to keep him on the jump is to screen off part of the road. Remember houses have carpets in them and clothes-lines, and a few of these put up as screens during the night so that behind them the attackers cross the street without being seen will play Hamlet with the Germans' nerves and ammunition supply.

They will also puzzle tanks, of which more anon.

STUDY THE WINDOWS

If you can attack houses on the side where there are fewest windows do so.

USE OF SMOKE

Smoke may be useful in the attack, but should SELDOM BE USED TO CONCEAL THE ATTACKERS.

Far better induce the enemy to think he is going to be attacked from one direction by putting down a smoke screen and then, when he is popping off into the smoke, attack him from another angle. Or you can mask his field of view with smoke while you advance, but if ever you have to attack in smoke make absolutely certain that all the men keep actually IN it, otherwise they will be presented to the enemy as black silhouettes against a white background (" presented " is a good word).

CROSSING A STREET

When a detachment is to cross a street under fire make sure it can get under cover at the other side. Move across one at a time unexpectedly, and if an automatic weapon is firing on the street time to get across whilst the magazine is being changed.

EXPLOSIVES WILL HELP

Explosives are useful for blowing in doors if there is someone in the party who understands them.

(NOTE.—A Mills grenade will NOT blow open a door.)

CHALK IS VERY USEFUL

When fighting in a maze of streets chalk marks and instructions written on the walls may be most useful, so every man in the patrol should have a piece of chalk, preferably coloured, so that each section can recognize its own information by the colour in which it is written.

STUDY THE MAP

Before the " schemozzle " a careful study of MAPS and photographs (both air and ground) will well repay the patrol.

HOW TO TACKLE A BARRICADE

In street fighting you may have to tackle a barricade and they are nasty things. If it is in any way possible to get round it, even at considerable trouble, do so rather than attack it from the front.

29

Covering fire against a barricade must be arranged from as high and close a spot as possible so as to get the bullets well down behind it. A mortar or a Northover projector is very useful. Sometimes barricades are made of inflammable material, and it is possible to set them on fire.

If you have to make a frontal attack try to mask the enemy with smoke, but do not attack in the first cloud. Let them blaze away into it. Then send over another and still do not go. Then send the third and storm the barricade.

X

DEFENDING HOUSES

I have first dealt with the attack in house-to-house fighting because for one thing ATTACK is the BEST DEFENCE, and for another if you master the technique of attack you have naturally fitted yourself to put up a good defence when necessary, because you know how your adversary is likely to act.

Suppose you are ordered to put some houses into a state of defence.

Here are some hints: —

WHICH WAY WILL THE HUN COME?

Before making your dispositions for defence put yourself in the enemy's place and say, " Now, how shall I attack these houses? Where shall I put my covering party? On which front shall I make my assault? "

The answers to these questions will give you valuable hints about the defence.

For instance, you might decide that a certain roof would be a good place from which to give covering fire, so when you worked out your defence scheme you would search for a spot where the defence could dominate it and so deny its use to the enemy.

30

PLATE 13

DO NOT LET YOUR BAYONET SHOW!

HOW TO APPROACH A CORNER.

HOW NOT TO LOOK ROUND

HOW TO LOOK ROUND.

WHENEVER POSSIBLE OCCUPY THE ROOF
(Provided it is flat and affords cover)

This will prevent the enemy from surprising you from that direction; it may also provide a good O.P. or a useful spot for snipers or bombers.

ALWAYS FIRE FROM UNEXPECTED PLACES

Remembering the enemy's covering fire, try to arrange things so that your own men can shoot from all sorts of unexpected places. If possible instead of from windows and doorways fire from loopholes cut at ground level, or from under the eaves. Sometimes houses which have basements have grids in the pavement. A man posted beneath one of those might have an interesting time if the enemy came sneaking along the side of the house.

It is an excellent principle to have far more loopholes than you have men and to change these in use periodically.

Dummy loopholes are invaluable and so are dummy heads to show in loopholes.

DON'T LET YOUR MUZZLE SHOW

All firing positions should be so arranged that a man can fire without his muzzle showing. Neglect of this simple precaution will cost precious lives. The German snipers are adept in the use of field-glasses and will all the time be studying your defences to see which loopholes to shoot at. The glint of a rifle muzzle will tell him all he wants to know.

GUARD AGAINST HAND GRENADES

Wire netting is the best defence and where there are houses there is usually some to be found. Up to two-inch mesh is quite effective. Cover windows, loopholes, etc., and any opening into which the enemy might hurl grenades. Failing wire netting, laths or boards nailed two inches apart will do quite well.

Glass should be removed from windows and they should all be made to look alike. Thin curtains often enable one to see without being seen.

DO NOT BE CAUGHT UNAWARES BY FIRE

As part of your defensive arrangements organize what fire-fighting equipment you can. You never know when or where incendiaries may appear in your defences. Inflammable material should be removed from the houses as much as possible and taken to a safe distance.

STRUT THE CELLARS

If you put up a stubborn defence you may get mortared or bombed from the air; consequently, it is wise to have somewhere extra strong to keep your ammunition, rations, water, candles, wounded, etc. If there is a garden or open ground near, a few slit trenches would be a wise precaution, but site them so that they are of no use to the enemy.

BARRICADE THE DOORS

All doors should be barricaded and the barricades should be covered by the fire of the defenders.

Keep one quick exit from the house in case you want to make a sortie or the place gets on fire.

CONNECT THE HOUSES

As soon as possible break openings in the dividing walls and connect up all the houses which are to be defended. This will help in all sorts of ways, from the movement of reinforcements and reliefs to the circulation of rations.

Loopholes between rooms may be useful if the enemy gets inside, but make them small, inconspicuous and in unexpected places or they may be a two-edged weapon.

BE SURE COVER IS BULLET-PROOF

If you have not got sandbags fill drawers and boxes with brick rubble or soil and reinforce the walls with them. Get a clear idea of what is bullet-proof and do not be satisfied with anything less.

Few walls of ordinary houses will withstand a burst of machine-gun fire at close range, and practically no floors are proof against small-arms fire from below.

ALLOCATE TO EVERY MAN HIS JOB

Be sure that every man knows what he should do in making the defences and what part he is to play if an attack. develops. Draw up a roster of look-out duties and see that the best possible O.P. is occupied.

CULTIVATE KEEN OBSERVATION

As part of your training for house-to-house fighting practise your powers of observation and deduction. A little thing changed, something not quite right, observed in time may save your life. Cultivate the habit of looking at everything critically, even ILLUSTRATIONS IN BOOKS, and you will find that your ability in this respect will rapidly develop.

LEARN TO SHOOT FROM BOTH SHOULDERS

An accomplishment fairly easily acquired is to shoot from the left shoulder as well as from the right. Practise it. It may make all the difference some time.

LOOK OUT FOR BOOBY TRAPS

If the enemy has been in occupation for any length of time LOOK OUT FOR BOOBY TRAPS. For some reason or other, the Germans take a childish delight in devising traps which will maim, blind or kill you if you are not careful, so while fighting from house to house do not touch a thing more than you need and be on your guard. If, for instance, you see in a house just left by the Germans a cat with its tail fast in a closed drawer don't yield to your first impulse to release it, but take the number of the house, wait till the battle is over and then send your mother-in-law to attend to it!

PLATE 14

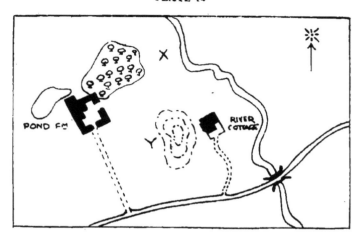

MUTUAL SUPPORT

In the above case, Patrol Leader wished to put a house in a state of defence, but he did not care much for POND FM., although it had clear fields of fire to N., W. and S., because there was a covered approach from the bed of the stream through the orchard right up to the farm buildings. From nowhere within the farm could fire be brought to bear on open ground at X.

Consequently, he went to RIVER COTTAGE, but here again there is a small hill behind which was ground Y which could not be covered from the cottage. If enemy got on to the hill he would dominate the cottage, so Patrol Leader was just about to look elsewhere when he had a *bright idea*. Why not defend them *both* and make them mutually supporting?

The cottage covered the approach at X and the farm covered the ground at Y.

This principle of MUTUAL SUPPORT is frequently applicable to defence of houses in built-up areas.

LITTLE THINGS WHICH MATTER

Trip wires with tins on them arranged to rattle and put in entries, back yards, etc., may give you welcome warning.

Barbed wire in doorways, etc., and dannert wire in entries can easily be made impenetrable obstacles and with a little ingenuity can be arranged to form a trap for the enemy.

Mills grenades and A.W. bombs have their uses in house-to-house fighting, but very careful judgment is required, as, for instance, a Mills grenade thrown upstairs may come rolling down again before it bursts, and a fire bomb may start a fire which cannot be put out.

Incidentally, when fighting in houses always move from cover to cover and every moment have in mind where you will dart should a grenade or a burst of fire come your way.

When approaching a corner take great care that your bayonet does not poke out before you look round.

XII

COMMON FAULTS

Before passing to some illustrations of house-to-house fighting I would like to indicate very clearly the faults to which fighting patrols are liable. This is so that you can look out for them and avoid them like the plague.

No. 1 FAULT—LACK OF DETERMINATION
Symptoms
- (a) A very long time is taken in coming to grips with enemy.
- (b) Exaggerated and prolonged use of cover.
- (c) Only a small number of attackers reach the objectives.
- (d) Heavy casualties.

36

Cause

(a) Plan of attack has not been made plain to all the men and consequently they are not sure where the enemy is or what is the limit of the patrol's attack, so naturally they hesitate.

(b) Faulty training. So much emphasis is often put on use of cover that some men get the idea that if they use plenty of cover they are doing their whack. A very comfortable idea to get, but fatal to fighting patrol tactics.

(c) When (b) happens only the hardiest spirits in the section get to grips with the enemy, and instead of there being ample numbers to dispose of them so many men are lagging behind that the attackers are in the *minority at the critical place and moment.*

(d) If for causes detailed above the action is spun out to over four times as long, that means that the enemy has four times the time in which to shoot at you. But it is worse than that because he can be calm and steady while he is doing it and much more accurate. Nothing disturbs the enemy's aim more than a well-covered, *steadily advancing* enemy. Nothing bucks him up more than to get the attackers tied down and reluctant to move.

No. 2 FAULT—LACK OF COHESION

Symptoms

(a) Men become spread out into couples or even single men widely separated and unable effectively to co-operate with one another.

(b) Parties supposed to do a pincer movement do not synchronize their final rush on to the enemy. Result is that enemy takes on each party in turn instead of being overwhelmed by a concerted assault.

37

Cause

(a) *Bad arrangement of tasks.* If men have a difficult route to traverse they should be allowed more time than men who can get straight there by an easy and sheltered approach.

(b) Sections have not been given a definite time by which to take up position for the final assault. Another cause is that the men have not been told what to do if something unexpected crops up, namely, to PUSH ON, WHATEVER HAPPENS.

(c) A signal to indicate the final charge should be arranged. All men should know it and from where to expect it.

No. 3 FAULT—LACK OF WARINESS

Symptoms

(a) The men are all so interested in scuppering the enemy in one house that every man's attention is riveted in that direction so that an enemy coming from anywhere else can surprise and take them at a terrible disadvantage.

(b) Whole detachment moves into cul-de-sac or goes into a house without guarding against an enemy closing the bottleneck.

(c) Men shout, talk and crash about, absolutely inviting enemy attention.

Cause

(a) Lack of IMAGINATION.

(b) Bad leadership and ignorance of elementary precautions.

(c) Carelessness and bad training.

WHENEVER THE FIGHTING PATROL IS IN BEING, NO MATTER WHERE IT IS OR WHAT IT IS DOING, SCOUTS SHOULD *ALWAYS* BE POSTED TO PROTECT IT AGAINST SURPRISE.

XIII

A STREET-FIGHTING
COMPETITION

The patrol was told : —

  (a) That a party of enemy was in occupation of
      the houses Y and Z on the plan (Plate 15).
  (b) That more enemy were expected at any
      moment.

Patrol was ordered : —

  (1) To destroy enemy.
  (2) To put Houses Y and Z in state of defence.
  (3) To block ASBURY ROAD against enemy
      coming from GREEN LANE.

The winning patrol advanced, with reasonable care,
along a quarter-mile of street, located, attacked and
ejected the enemy, erected a road block of dannert wire
and cylinders, and took up defensive positions within
forty-five minutes.

This was a good performance and the way the patrol
moved, with scouts protecting it on front, flank *and* rear
showed they had been well trained.

Covering fire was well directed and the attack was
conducted without hesitation or delay.

Lessons brought out by the competition : —

  (1) In this street fighting, just as in all fighting
  patrol operations, the worst failing is the tendency
  for the patrol to split up into a lot of ineffective
  parts wandering aimlessly up entries and through
  gardens. THE PATROL MUST BE CAPABLE
  OF DELIVERING A HARD COLLECTIVE
  PUNCH AT THE END.

  There were twelve enemy in Houses Y and Z,
  and one patrol after a long time succeeded in getting FOUR men into the houses, and nobody
  followed to back them up! That sort of action is
  no use. The patrol consisted of twenty-five men,
  ample to scupper twelve Germans, but where were
  they? A few were giving covering fire, so to that

39

PLATE 15

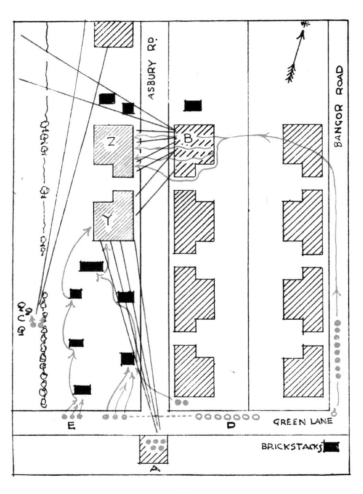

40

extent could be counted part of the " punch," but the bulk of the patrol, who should have been setting about the invaders, were lying behind walls, hiding in buildings and generally doing nothing at all to defend democracy. The Leader had completely lost them and they apparently had no orders to push on to the objective.

Another patrol after sixty minutes had shown no signs of getting to grips.

In all operations such as this SPEED IN CLOSING WITH THE ENEMY IS OF PARAMOUNT IMPORTANCE and almost everything else is a minor matter. Incidentally, a lot of time was wasted by men creeping with the greatest possible precaution and slowness over ground which had already been safely traversed by several scouts.

When moving along a road protected by scouts the patrol should keep close together unless actually fired upon.

(2) Immediately the Patrol Leader received information that Germans were close to he should have thrown out protective scouts WITHOUT A SECOND'S DELAY. For all he knew, the enemy was following up the civilian who brought the news. Any streets the enemy might cross and all entries, etc., from which attack could come should be carefully watched by scouts.

(3) Quietness is essential if casualties are to be avoided. For instance, one patrol decided to give covering fire from B to Z, *i.e.*, from very close to the enemy. Obviously the covering party should have crept upstairs as stealthily as stoats because they knew the enemy was established in .the bedrooms opposite. Instead of that the clump! clump! clump! of their heavy boots could be heard 100 yards away as they pounded their way upstairs, absolutely presenting their lives to the enemy.

In two cases the instructions of the Patrol Leader for the final attack were issued so loudly that the enemy could hear them all; and doubtless found them helpful!

(4) After capturing the houses several patrols at once set about blocking the road without first arranging an adequate look-out and without leaving anyone to defend the houses; this in spite of the information given at the outset " that more enemy were expected at any moment."

(5) So far as my observations went, not one patrol sent back word to the Company Commander after the objective was captured.

SOLUTION

Here is a solution (notice I do not say " the " solution, because sometimes these tactical problems have several solutions equally good). I give it in the form of orders as they should be issued by the Patrol Leader after he has called his three Section Leaders together at D.

" No. 1 SECTION.—You will provide covering fire for No. 3 Section, who will attack from the south—that is, from GREEN LANE. Take four men to house at bottom of ASBURY ROAD, south of GREEN LANE (A).

" Go through the gardens at the back and when you get there keep very quiet till No. 3 Section is ready to advance by bounds from brickstack to brickstack. When you see they are ready plaster the enemy with rapid fire while No. 3 Section gets across. Send two men along the hedge (C) west of the houses : —

" (1) To snipe any enemy they see.
" (2) To look out for hostile reinforcements from the west.
" (3) To bump off any Huns running away.

" After houses are taken you will leave a look-out in the house A and use the rest of your section as a protective screen round Houses Y and Z whilst rest of patrol is blocking the road."

" No. 3 SECTION.—You will attack the Houses Y

42

and Z from GREEN LANE under covering fire from
No. 1 Section. Wait here till No. 1 Section is ready and
then cross to cover of the low wall at E. From there
advance by bounds from brickstack to brickstack.

"After houses have been captured your section will
at once block the road between the houses.

"Commence advance in ten minutes from word
'Move.'"

"No. 2 SECTION.—You have heard what One and
Three Sections are going to do. You will take No. 2
Section along BANGOR ROAD, and, keeping well
under cover, cross the gardens to the fourth block of
houses UP ASBURY ROAD from GREEN LANE
(B).

"Put out a couple of men to give covering fire across
ASBURY ROAD, and when you hear No. 3 Section
attack go all out for House Z.

"After the Houses Y and Z are captured you will at
once start putting them in a state of defence."

"All three sections must be in a position to start ten
minutes from now. If something comes unstuck push
on at all costs and don't wait for anything.

"Any questions? MOVE!"

XIV

TANKS IN TOWNS

Tanks will never come close to houses if they can
be avoided; but sometimes they will have to come and
then is the opportunity of the defence.

They should be assailed by every weapon available,
and the attack should continue till the tank is definitely
worsted. The entry of a tank into a built-up area
should be the sign for rifles, shot-guns, Mills grenades,
A.W. bombs, Molotoff cocktails, flame-throwers and
anti-tank mines to get busy.

A shot-gun against a tank does not sound very
effective, but it keeps its lid down and a small pellet
may penetrate a visor when a bullet would not enter,
and at such places is usually a pig-like eye.

43

Every effort should be made to slow it down by screens (made of carpets, sheets and clothes-lines) and obstacles, such as cars, carts and regular road blocks, and where it will slow down *there* should be the flames, the bullets and the explosives. Do not be disappointed if the tank does not immediately respond to treatment, but KEEP IT UP and you will win. REMEMBER THIS—if you can keep touch with a German tank till it goes dark it is helpless and easy meat.

The motto for those fighting tanks amongst houses is "*Keep ABOVE it or keep BELOW it.*" Should a tank succeed in getting past your defences don't worry, just sit tight and get ready for the next one.

When the Germans come they will go all out to crush us in one awful rush and they will stake everything on their ability to overcome us quickly. If after their armoured troops have passed on all sorts of determined men spring up in all sorts of places and fight and fight and FIGHT regardless of what is happening elsewhere the Germans will be helpless adequately to supply or reinforce their forward troops and Nemesis will be upon them.

X V

CONCLUSION

TO FIGHT SUCCESSFULLY AMONGST HOUSES REQUIRES TWO THINGS—KNOWLEDGE OF THE UNDERLYING PRINCIPLES AND *practice*.

IF YOU HAVE FOLLOWED ME CLOSELY THROUGH THE FOREGOING YOU HAVE THE KNOWLEDGE, SO *now* FOR THE PRACTICE.

GO TO IT AND WHILE YOU PRACTISE USE YOUR IMAGINATION AND TRY ACTUALLY TO *see* YOUR ENEMY IN EVERY NOOK AND CORNER.

MAKE YOUR PRACTICE INTO A GREAT GAME, FOR THAT IS WHAT HOUSE-TO-HOUSE FIGHTING REALLY IS.

Lightning Source UK Ltd.
Milton Keynes UK
UKHW020305211020
371937UK00005B/49